# FRIENDSHIP

## GUIDE FOR FRIENDS

JIYA R. SHAH

This book is dedicated to all your friends. And to the people who are someone's friends.

# Contents

# Preface

## ABOUT THE BOOK

Books are our first friends. They make us happy, teach us good things and comfort us with their words just like friends. This book gives us guidance for friendship. It helps us find good friends and helps to identify fake friends and enemies. Gives guidance in maintaining a good friendship. It's a complete guide to friendship. I thought of friendship and betrayal and wrote down my thoughts for you. I have taken the reference of the subject material about the title friendship from Google also which may be noted.

JIYA R. SHAH

# CHAPTER ONE

# LIFE IS LIKE A....

LIFE IS LIKE A CIRCLE
   WHAT IS DONE BY US
   ALWAYS COMES BACK TO US
   SOONER OR LATER ONE
   HAS TO PAY FOR IT

   LIFE IS LIKE AN OPPORTUNITY
   GIVING ONE CHANCE TO
   IMPROVE OR REMAKE SOMETHING
   DEEDS DONE ARE BEING A
   MISTAKE OR A MIRACLE?

   LIFE IS LIKE A CHALLENGE
   ASKING IF YOU CAN MAKE IT OR NOT
   BUT ALWAYS EXPECT YOU TO WIN
   LIFE IS LIFE ALWAYS GIVEN ONCE
   SPEND IT WISELY OR YOU GONNA
   BE THE REGRETTING ONES

# CHAPTER TWO

# ARE YOU HAPPY?

LIFE IS TO BE HAPPY
  SO BE HAPPY
  NO MATTER HOW MANY
  PROBLEMS YOU TOLERATED

FORGET THEM AND MOVE ON
IF NOT THEN YOU ARE A MORON
THINKING ABOUT WHAT HAPPENED IN PAST
WASTE BECAUSE NOW IT DOESN'T LAST
THINKING ABOUT PRESENT
WILL SHOW WAY TO ENLIGHTENMENT
MAKING OTHERS HAPPY
IS THE BEST WORK

BEING HAPPY IS THE BEST EMOTION
ALWAYS SMILING IS THE BEST EXPRESSION
TOLERATING PAIN IS YOUR COMPULSION
BUT FORGETTING IT DOES NOT REQUIRE
PERMISSION

# CHAPTER THREE

# TIME TO MAKE A FRIEND

MAKE THEM WISELY BECAUSE SOMETIMES THINGS DONE IN HASTE ARE OFTEN GONE WASTE ALWAYS KNOW A PERSON BEFORE BEING A FRIEND BECAUSE IN TODAY'S WORLD BETRAYAL IS A WELL KNOWN TREND

DON'T SHARE VERY MUCH WITH YOUR FRIENDS YOU NEVER KNOW ARE YOUR SECRETS IN GOOD HANDS THE PERSON SHOULD UNDERSTAND & BEHAVE WELL OTHERWISE WE MIGHT REGRET OURSELVES TELL

REGRETTING OUR DECISION IS NOT THE OPTION IT'S TIME TO BREAK THE TOGETHER CONNECTION IF YOUR MIND SAYS THE PERSON IS NOT TRUSTABLE THEN YOU ARE SAVED FROM BEING A BETRAYAL SAMPLE

# CHAPTER FOUR

# IS IT OK TO GET BETRAYED?

It is ok to get betrayed. Getting betrayed is a normal stage of life that everyone has gone through at least once. The person giving the betrayal is doing wrong, but getting betrayed isn't someone's fault. It's hard to know how it feels until you experience it yourself. Betrayal is among the most. devastating losses a person can experience. We live in a culture that is blind to betrayal and intolerant of emotional pain. Loss happens in many experiences and circumstances, and it can affect us deeply. The one who has been betrayed is grieving. Whether the aftermath is expressed through apologies or being ignored, betrayal hurts like hell. We can heal, but it will have to be in our own time and on our terms.

After being betrayed, most of us want two things, usually at the same time. We want to wound the person who hurt us—as deeply and as excruciatingly—as we've been wounded, and we want to rise above the situation and offer that person forgiveness. But neither of these tactics works. Wounding words tend to boomerang and make you feel as terrible as the person you wanted to hurt. Forgiveness, especially if halfhearted, tends to come off as condescension.

There are actions, though, that you can take to can heal yourself. Every hurt has its own story, and so does every healing. But we can say this: You can heal yourself when you've filled the hole left behind by a betrayal, and you can heal the other person when you sincerely drop the need for revenge.

Remember, the only betrayals that inflict damage are the ones where an intimate bond has been torn. Love makes you merge with another person, able to feel their emotions as keenly as you feel your own. If you have experienced such bonding, you know that it is a kind of higher reality—and when that bond is ripped apart, it's as if you've lost half of yourself.

# CHAPTER FIVE

# ARE THEY, MY FRIENDS?

We've all had friendships that have ended up a little pear-shaped and it's unfortunate that most of the time, we all have to get burnt before we can spot a bad friend from a good one. Finding real friends is a very difficult task, this chapter will help you identify real and fake, friends or enemies.

1. All friendships should be equal – which means that you should receive as much as you put in, it's all based on reciprocation and mutuality. If you're putting in more than you're getting out, you should think twice about what they are asking from you. Some friends only call when they need something not more than that, For them, you are not a friend but just a backup to ask something. They are not friends.

2. Do you find that you just spend your whole time focused on them when you're hanging out? Yeah, that's not cool – we all have problems and things we'd like to talk to somebody about. Friends who just do not let you speak, and expect you to hear are not real. The conversation is never equal. It shows for them you are a listener, nothing else. They just want someone to hear them not to speak. They

are not friends.

3. Have your friends ever put you down or made fun of you in front of others? Are these types of people called a friend? A definite no-no. Usually, people do this because they feel bad about themselves and want to use somebody else as a distraction. Draw a line through any friendships like this immediately. They don't like someone saying good of you instead of them. Not friends at all.

4. They never share anything with you. The opposite is also true. If you find yourself constantly opening up to your friend and sharing your deepest secrets with them, but they never return the favor, they may not consider you a close enough friend to trust you. Sure, some people find it harder to open up than others, but if your life is an open book and their life is kept under lock and key, then things are seriously one-sided and that's not what true friendships are about.

5. They judge you. It's one thing for your friend to be honest and offer you constructive criticism (like when she tells you it's probably not a good idea to get close to that guy you're crushing on even if he is giving you mixed signals). But if you're scared to talk to your friend about certain things because they're constantly judging you and making you feel bad about your choices, they probably aren't your best friend.

6. They're never happy for you.

Your besties should be your biggest fans. So if you feel like your friend never has anything nice to say when you achieve something, or worse, they try to one-up you instead of congratulating you, it's a sign they see you as competition, not a friend. Sure, sometimes you and your friend will like the same guy or go out for the same part in the play, and things might get a little competitive and awkward between you, but your friendship shouldn't feel like a constant competition

7. They constantly dish your secrets in front of other people.

It's understandable to slip up and accidentally reveal a secret every once and a while when you and your friend run in the same circles, but if your friend is constantly apologizing for "accidentally" revealing a secret that you asked them to keep between you, they're probably not the most trustworthy friend. Either they like gossiping or they just have a blabbermouth and your secrets probably aren't safe with them.

Make friends who are your friends and care for you. It's easy to find enemies in form of friends, but really hard to find real friends

# CHAPTER SIX

# NO FRIENDS (ALONE)

Making friends can be a difficult task in this day and age. Some people just do not know how to adjust their personalities so that they can fit in with others and make acquaintances You may see someone that seems likable and appears like they are a decent person, only to find out that they have almost no social life.

The truth is that you can't tell if someone is a loner just by looking at them. You may not even be able to figure it out from just your first meeting or interaction with them. It's easy for most of us to make friends, but we might think of those who find it an important test of life.

They like to be alone rather than have friends. Have you ever heard that someone went to a restaurant alone? Or goes alone to watch movies. It might be weird for you to hear about this type of situation because most of us go with our friends or people we know to this type of place.

People who are alone with no friends are very rarely seen with someone. One giveaway for those who would be a loner is that they will often separate themselves from groups of other people and prefer keeping to themselves. People who don't have friends and always aim to isolate themselves tend to not have very many friends. They don't have friends, but it doesn't mean they don't want to make one. They just find it difficult to make friends or to merge with someone. If you notice that they never open up a conversation with you or other people and actively avoid being the first one to speak. They don't like to talk that much. It is normal for anyone to be alone. This shows how much they are open to someone or how much they love themselves. But we all should also be this capacity to don't need someone to help us, comfort us, or make us happy. All might need a person to do this thing and you should have a person who thinks of you. But just develop a thing in case you are alone, you should know how to handle it.

# HOW TO MAKE FRIENDS?

Friends are wonderful. They make you laugh, they go on adventures with you, and they're there for you when times are tough. But sometimes making new friends can feel hard, whether you're trying to meet friends in school, online, or as an adult. Fortunately, making new friends doesn't have to be hard, especially once you know where to look and how to put yourself out there. Keep reading to learn foolproof tips and strategies for making new friends so you can start building the friendships you deserve. If you want to make friends, you first need to put yourself out there somehow to meet people. If you just sit alone, friends might come to you, but that's not likely because they might think you want to stay alone

"Good friends bring so many colors of happiness in your life by relieving stress, giving comfort, and removing loneliness," says Amber O'Brien, PsyD, a psychologist with the Mango Clinic in Miami.

Healthy friendships are also linked to better cardiovascular health, lower blood pressure, less depression, and longer life. So it never hurts to try to make new friends.

Join an organization or club to meet new people. This is a great way to find other people who have common interests. You don't necessarily need to have a lot of common interests with people to make friends with them. Sometimes children can be anxious about what they will play with other kids ("What will we do?!"). Take out a piece of paper and make a list of five or more games that your child would like to play with someone else. This way they are ready to go up and ask someone to play a game with them, or they are prepared with some ideas if someone new comes up to them. Friendliness, and the confidence to make friends, are important for all children to develop so they can get along with others. Sometimes as adults who have had so many experiences meeting new people, we may forget how hard it can be for our kids to put themselves out there and talk to people they do not know. We may not give a second thought to a situation where we need to make a new friend if a best friend is absent, but this may feel like a huge deal to our young child.

It's easy to make friends, first try to merge with them. People having the same interests and personalities are easy to be friends with.

# CHAPTER EIGHT

# ARE YOU A GOOD FRIEND?

There's a friend in mind as I write this. She's more a sister than a friend. How I lucked into such an amazing human being is .beyond me, but I did, and it's wonderful This connection wasn't simply pulled from the ether, nor does it maintain itself by sparkles and rainbows.

Certain qualities must be shared to form the bonds of good and true friendship. Friends aren't those who bow down and tolerate, they aren't the ones giving sacrifices too, nor the ones to be framed for everything. True friends are the ones who give always the right advice and reviews.

1. They're Kind

You'd think this was a given for any type of human interaction, but kindness is often overlooked.

We've likely experienced that "bend over backward" kind of kindness that, to be honest, makes people a little uncomfortable.

The kindness of a good friend is more of the "stand with you" variety. Rather than give you the shirt off their back, they'll make sure that both of your needs are tended to so that there's never a need for you to get stressed.

2. They're Honest

Another of the main qualities of a good friend is that they will let you know when they're hurt by you, confused by you, see you being foolish, and can tell when you're hiding.

A lot of people don't want to do any of these. It's easier for them to hide behind "I don't want to hurt your feelings."

Thing is, good friends, share. Even pain. Discomfort enters everywhere in life; it'd be dishonest to pretend it avoids friendship altogether.

3. They're Individual

A sense of identity creates amazing bonds. Good friends aren't trying to become you, they're fully realized unto themselves.

Their sense of individuality plays off your own, and even enhances areas in both of you that may have gone unnoticed before.

And while dreams, goals, and temperaments are often similar, even the best symbiotic friendships know there are times when each individual must pull away to reflect and rejuvenate on their own.

4. They're Adventurous

Boredom is the absence of stimulation, be it mental, emotional, or physical stimulation.

Good friends satisfy all three of those areas; they're adventurous in that they like to do things, think things, feel things, and share those things with you.

This doesn't necessarily mean mountain climbing or bungee jumping; a trip to a new restaurant will do.

The desire and willingness to experience the world is an inseparable part of friendship because it says "take my hand and let's see what's out there!"

5. They're playful.

Friends play with us. They make us laugh at the most inopportune moments (devils) and catching a twinkle in their eyes is like the promise of Christmas morning.

The world pretends to be a serious place, but playtime stops it dead in its tracks every time. Good friends know how the world is, but they also know how to cheer you up by playing to forget the serious world and step out.

They always are playful when you are getting bored, remember each thing and games of your favorites. They always know your interests and likes.

6. They're Protective

Jimi Hendrix was probably thinking about a good friend when he came up with the lyric, "I stand up next to a mountain, I chop it down with the edge of my hand."

Good friends aren't protective of you in a self-interested, possessive way; they're protective of you, all the oddly shaped, precious, intrinsic bits that make up your traveling soul because those are the bits that truly gravitationally attract us to bright, brilliant souls.

It is a mission they take upon themselves often without knowing they've done so, but they'll do it from here to eternity, whether standing up to a mountain, shielding you from impending harm, or even at times protecting you from yourself.

7. They're Trustworthy

There are people we trust only as far as we see them. Those don't make good friends.

Then there are those whom we'd place everything that makes us "us" into an egg, give it to them, and allow them to race on pogo sticks across a booby-trapped, rubble-strewn field while we sip lemonade during the wait for them to return it.

We trust our good friends to be good people. If not: splat.

8. They're Nurturing

Yes, a good friend holds your hair aside for you while you are making a painting, but she also makes sure you're eating enough, getting enough rest, sinking into bubble baths at least once a month, and listening wide-eyed as you recount to her your latest achievement or newfound goal.

Good friends become friends, parents, lovers, doctors, and confidants all in one without it ever seeming hard.

9. They Listen

Compassion and empathy combine to make our good friends excellent listeners because, honestly, who wants to project "Me, me, me" all the time at anyone?

It's good to be silent and allow our friends to fill us with themselves, as they do with us.

Another key characteristic of a good friend is that they listen to your hopes, fears, questions, dreams, foolishness, musings, prattlings, and more, not out of obligation, but because they genuinely care.

10. They're Helpful

A good friend has your back. Not in a pinch. Always.

If you're tired, they take on your load. If you need help figuring something out, they're your research partners. They neither tally nor begrudge, and if one task is done and you need them for more, they have no problem being there. Period.

They always do your things whenever you ask or they feel it. Helping is the best quality of a good friend.

11. They're Respectful

Respectful of you, respectful of your time, respectful of your right to make mistakes: these are hallmarks of someone worthy of being allowed into your life.

Respectful of the things you love, the things you fear, the things you avoid. Without respect, friendship slips into becoming just another of narcissism's mirrors: you see the other as little more than an extension of you until they're no longer useful. Always respect our ideas, help us improve our thinking, and give good advice.

12. They're Open-Hearted

Friendship is like an extreme sport of soul-to-soul connectivity: we're slamming about on this Earth never knowing where we'll bounce or who these people we bounce off of are. Extreme human.

It takes guts to open yourself to someone who feels as randomly placed on a planet as you do. But good friends do this. They open their hearts, bare their souls, and leave space for you to tuck away a piece of yourself in there for safekeeping.

It's a long journey, this extreme human; good friends not only make the trip bearable, but they also transform it into a rowdy, wild, absolute delight.

13. They Will Forgive You For (Almost) Anything

One of the most important qualities of a good friend is that they will do everything they can to forgive you when you do wrong by them. They will try to understand the reasons you acted as you did, they will talk to you about it, and they will try and help you resolve any troubles you may be facing.

That's not to say that they will let you get away with absolutely anything. It is possible to destroy friendships with a single act, no matter how true and deep they are.

They may well forgive you for what you have done even if they decide that it is best to part ways.

14. You Feel Comfortable Enough To Ask Them A Favor

Relating closely back to the point on someone's willingness to help, if you would be happy to ask someone for a favor, there's every chance you consider that person a close friend.

This is because you are confident that they will do whatever they can to assist you and because should they not be able to help, you won't take it as a rejection. If you ask a more casual acquaintance for a favor and they say no, you may well be left wondering what their reasons are. At last, these are the qualities a good friend should have. There are many more but I gave as many main things as I can.

# CHAPTER NINE

# HOW TO MAINTAIN FRIENDSHIP?

In maintaining friendship most important thing is, that friends should understand each other. Supporting and trust are the main elements of maintaining a friendship. Without any friendship doesn't last long. Here are some tips for you to maintain a good and healthy friendship.

1) Create and capitalize on time together.

Of course, it's nice to have those friendships that don't require a lot of time or upkeep—especially when the two of you are miles and miles apart or on opposite schedules. That being said, however, strong relationships do require staying in touch and spending meaningful time together. So, at the very least, check in with your friend when you can: agree on weekly phone dates; text them here and there to let them know you're thinking of them; and if possible, schedule some time to simply hang out.

2) Be honest with each other.

Another key to strengthening your friendships is being open and honest with your friends. "When conflict arises in healthy relationships, both people can listen intently to each other as they express the way they feel," says Psychotherapist Dena Alley. You need to be able to express how you feel—even those negative feelings like disappointment and discomfort—to keep that bond from weakening. If you instead keep those feelings bottled up, you're likely to foster some ill will towards your friends, and your relationships will suffer. So instead of brushing how you feel under the rug, confront your emotions openly. Then, you can work out the issue together.

3) Show them that you care.

If you hope to create strong, lasting friendships, you should continue to show your friend that you care about them. This doesn't require you to take drastic measures, but simply find ways to express your love and appreciation for the other person: treat them to pizza on their birthday; tag them in cheesy memes on Facebook, and bluntly tell them that your friendship means the world to you. You might assume that they already know you care for them, but even if they do, it's always nice to be reminded

4) BITS OF ADVICE AND THOUGHTS

Clear what you have in your mind for them or something related to them. Give good advice, this makes friendship stronger.

5) Embark on new experiences together.

Licensed Psychologist Dr. Wyatt Fisher says, "an essential ingredient to a strong relationship is having fun with the person." Relationships are strengthened by meaningful experiences and unforgettable memories. So make the effort to spice up your friendships by embarking on new adventures side-by-side: sign up for an intimidating exercise or cooking class together; plan a trip to a new town or even a new country; or simply switch up your typical weekend outings. This variation will revive your friendships and create an even stronger bond.

6) SPEND TIME WITH EACH OTHER.

You will know each other better as well as understand better. Create or take advantage of opportunities to meet their significant others, relatives, cherished family members, and other friends. Develop common hobbies and mutual interests or learn about the activities they enjoy and what makes them come alive.

7)Provide support and encouragement.

Friendships aren't all fun and games—they do require you to put in some work, such as when your friend is having a horrible, no-good day. It's your job to be there for them and provide them with whatever they need, starting with support and comfort. Additionally, you must encourage them as needed. Encourage them to do what you know will make them happy, like taking that job or moving to a new city. Whatever the case, make it apparent that you're rooting for them.

8) Treasure the little things.

Real, strong friendships aren't extravagant—they're built simply on connectedness, kindness, and love for each other. That being said, you must remember to embrace and rejoice in the little things. Appreciate those phone dates we talked about earlier. Enjoy every second you get to spend with them, even if you're simply meeting for coffee. Treasure every little piece of your friendship—the extraordinary love, the undying support, and the irreplaceable memories.

# CHAPTER TEN

# MOM IS MY FRIEND

Moms are our friends technically, they do everything a friend does. In this chapter, you will learn and understand if your mom is your friend or not. List of things moms do as a friend-

1)Make us happy like friends.

2)Comfort us like them

3)Scold if we have done something wrong

4)Give good and valuable advice.

5)Explain each thing clearly.

6)Spend time with us.

7)Save us from everyone's scoldings.

8)Give a perfect reply to people who give free statements about us.

Moms are our first friends. Friends may come and friends may go but your mom is always by your side. Friends maybe give wrong advice to you but mom always gives correct advice. Even so, it's not impossible to become friends with your parents. "If parents can recognize that their child is a grownup, they can enjoy a true friendship. Turns out there's a good reason for that: mother-daughter relationships are the strongest of all parent-child bonds, according to a study published in the Journal of Neuroscience. The research found that mothers and daughters are more likely to understand and relate to the emotions of each other than anyone else. What we do as friends with our moms

1)We share things with mom.

2)Spend time with them.

3)Help them

4) Make them happy and comfort them.

Yes, you can be friends with your mom. It is the best decision.No one knows you better than your mom. Spend time with her, make her happy, and give them comfort. This increases your friendship you get a chance to know your mom.

www.ingramcontent.com/pod-product-compliance
Lightning Source LLC
Chambersburg PA
CBHW061410160726
47995CB00002B/542